Exploring Space

The Milky Way

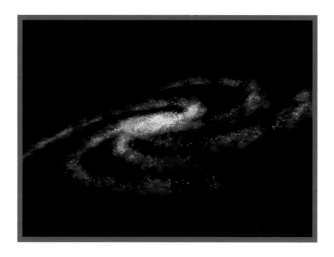

by Martha E. H. Rustad

Consulting Editor: Gail Saunders-Smith, PhD

Consultant: Ilia Iankov Roussev, PhD
Associate Astronomer & Associate Professor
Institute for Astronomy, University of Hawaii at Manoa

CAPSTONE PRESS
a capstone imprint

Pebble Plus is published by Capstone Press,
1710 Roe Crest Drive, North Mankato, Minnesota 56003.
www.capstonepub.com

Books published by Capstone Press are manufactured with paper
containing at least 10 percent post-consumer waste.

Library of Congress Cataloging-in-Publication Data
Rustad, Martha E. H. (Martha Elizabeth Hillman), 1975–
 The milky way / by Martha E. H. Rustad.
   p. cm.—(Pebble plus. Exploring space)
 Includes bibliographical references and index.
 Summary: "Full-color photographs and simple text provide a brief introduction to the Milky Way galaxy"—Provided by
publisher.
 ISBN 978-1-4296-7583-3 (library binding)
 ISBN 978-1-4296-7893-3 (paperback)
 1. Milky Way—Juvenile literature. I. Title.
 QB857.7.R87 2012
 523.1'13—dc23   2011021648

Editorial Credits
Erika L. Shores, editor; Alison Thiele, designer; Kathy McColley, production specialist

Photo Credits
iStockphoto/Rick Whitacre, 5
NASA, 19, GSFC, 1, JPL-Caltech, 11, cover, JPL-Caltech/R. Hurt (SSC), 21
NASA/Robert Williams and the Hubble Deep Field Team (STScI), 18
newscom/xinhua/Xinhua/Photoshot, 13
Photolibrary/Peter Arnold Images/Detlev van Ravenswaay, 15
Photo Researchers, Inc/Mark Garlick, 17
Shutterstock/Sander van Sinttruye, 7
X-ray: NASA/CXC/CfA/M.Markevitch et al.; Optical: NASA/STScI; Magellan/U.Arizona/D.Clowe et al.; Lensing Map:
    NASA/STScI; ESO WFI; Magellan/U.Arizona/D.Clowe et al., 9

Artistic Effects
Shutterstock: glossygirl21, Primož Cigler, SmallAtomWorks

Note to Parents and Teachers

The Exploring Space series supports national science standards related to earth science.
This book describes and illustrates the Milky Way. The images support early readers in
understanding the text. The repetition of words and phrases helps early readers learn new
words. This book also introduces early readers to subject-specific vocabulary words, which are
defined in the Glossary section. Early readers may need assistance to read some words and to
use the Table of Contents, Glossary, Read More, Internet Sites, and Index sections of the book.

Printed in the United States of America in North Mankato, Minnesota.
102011   006405CGS12

Table of Contents

What Is the Milky Way?

Look at the night sky.

Can you see a thick band

of light? This wavy white path

is called the Milky Way.

The Milky Way is our galaxy.

A galaxy is a huge group of

stars, planets, dust, and gas.

We can see only part of

our galaxy in the night sky.

The Milky Way has about
200 billion stars. Our Sun is
one of those stars. Astronomers
think there are hundreds of
billions of galaxies in the universe.

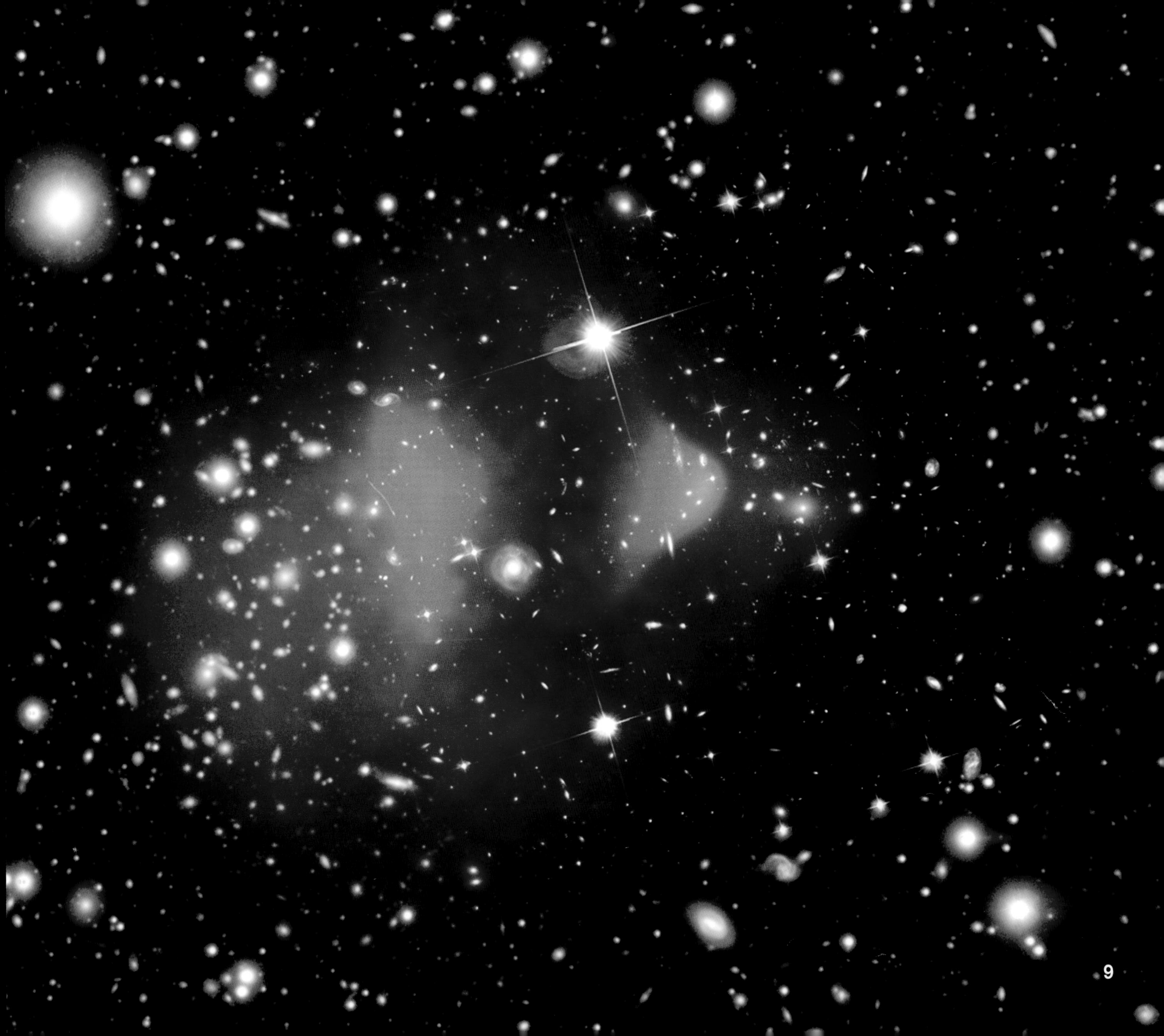

Shape and Size

The Milky Way is shaped
like a pinwheel.
In the middle is a big bulge.
Spiral arms spread out
from the middle.

Our Sun is in one of
the spiral arms.
It is about halfway out
from the center.

Sun

The Milky Way is very big.
Light takes about 100,000 years
to travel across it. Light takes
about 1,000 years to travel
from top to bottom.

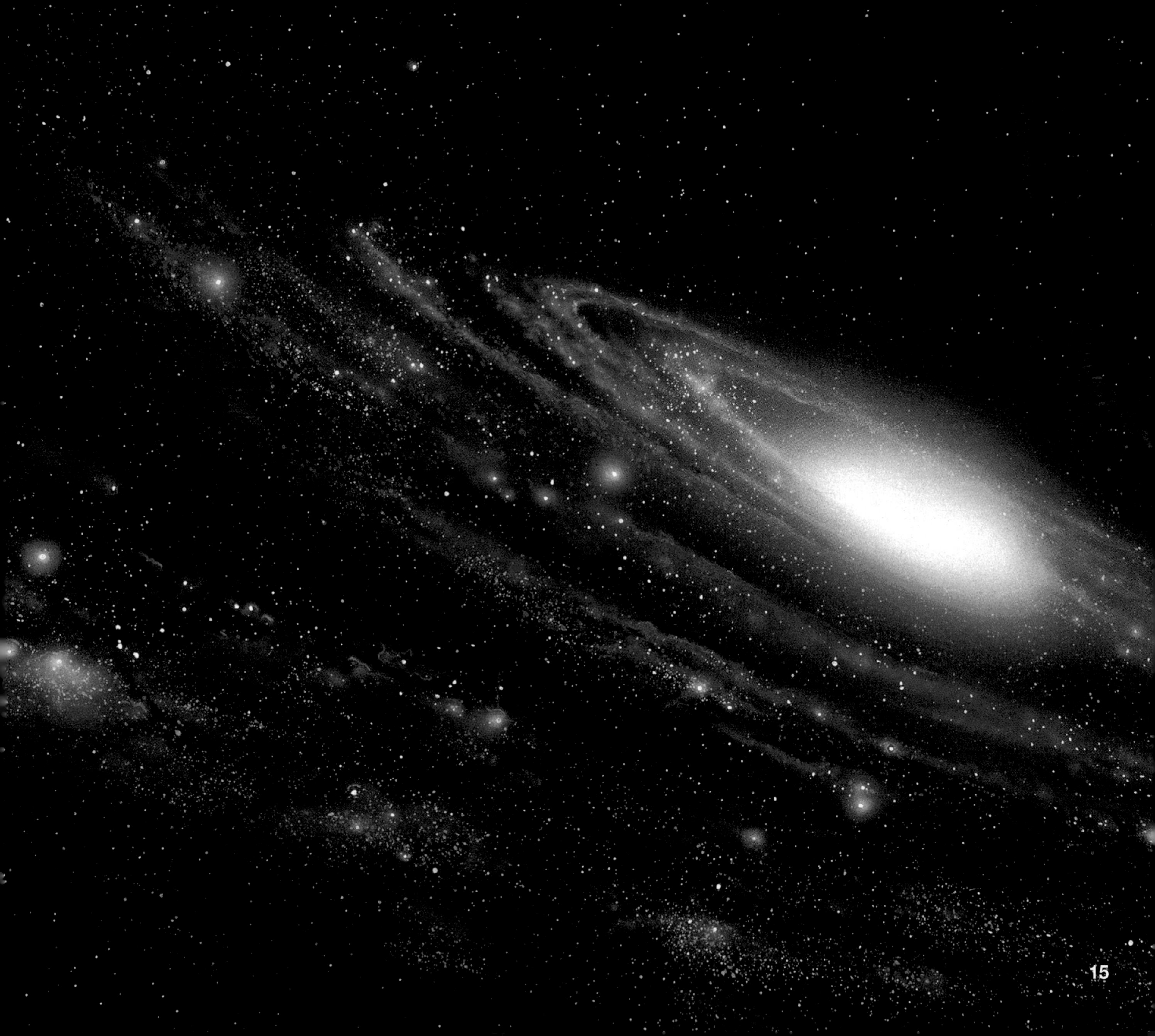

The Milky Way turns very slowly. The Sun makes a complete trip around the center every 226 million years. Earth follows the Sun around the galaxy.

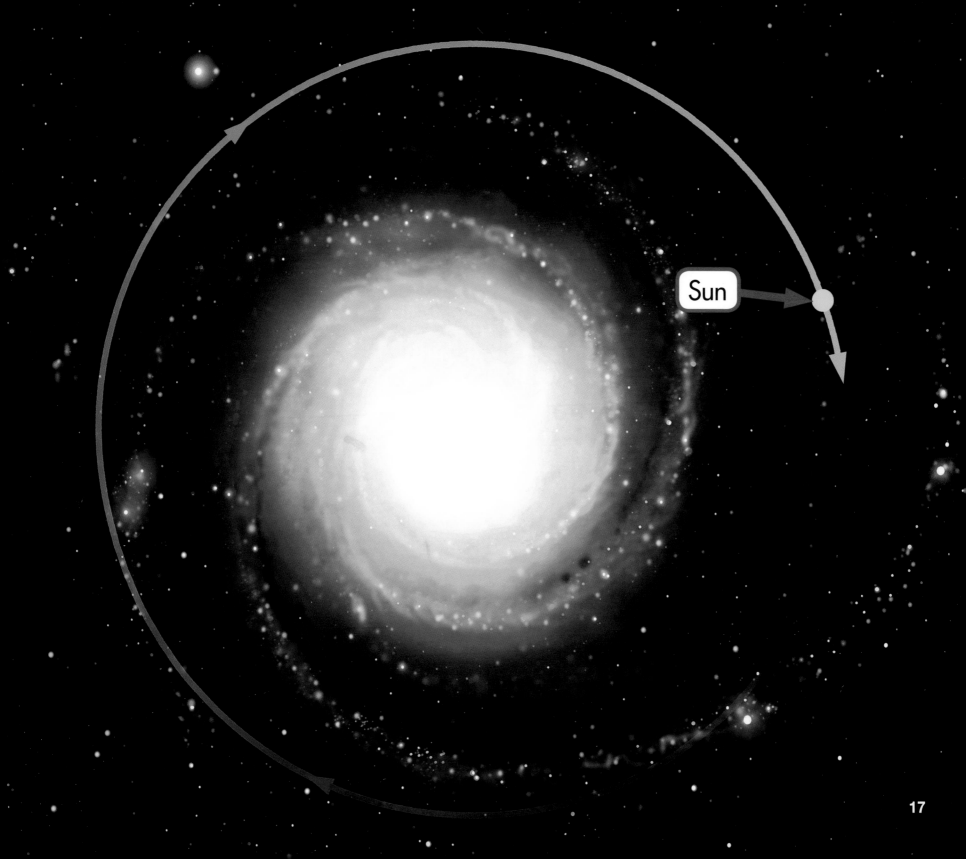

Sun

Studying the Milky Way

Astronomers look at other galaxies to learn about the Milky Way. Powerful telescopes in space take pictures of far off stars and galaxies.

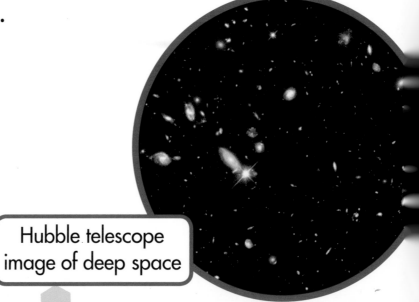

Hubble telescope image of deep space

Astronomers use telescopes
to help make maps of
our galaxy. Because we are
inside it, we cannot take pictures
of the entire Milky Way.

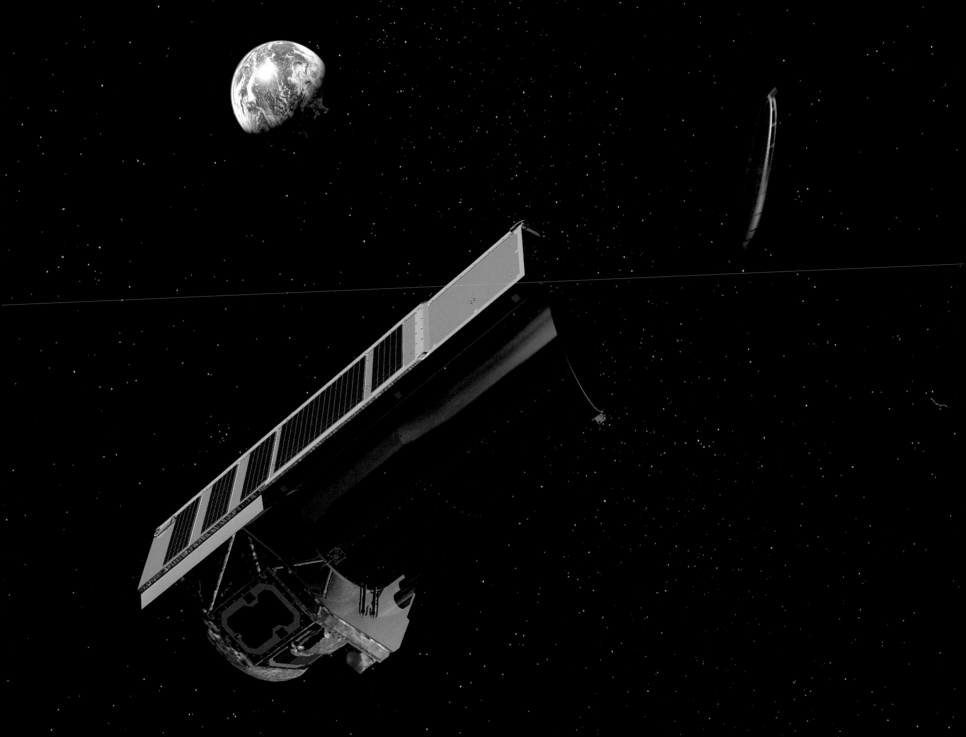

Glossary

astronomer—a scientist who studies stars, planets, and other objects in space

galaxy—a large group of billions of stars, planets, dust, and gas

spiral—a pattern of circles getting wider and wider

star—a ball of hot, bright gases in space; the Sun is a star

telescope—a tool people use to look at planets and other objects in space; telescopes make planets and other objects look closer than they really are

universe—everything that exists, including Earth, the planets, the stars, and all of space

Read More

Howard, Fran. *The Milky Way.* The Universe. Edina, Minn.: ABDO Pub. Co., 2008.

Jefferis, David. *Galaxies: Immense Star Islands.* Exploring Our Solar System. New York: Crabtree Pub., 2009.

Kortenkamp, Steve. *The Milky Way.* The Solar System. Mankato, Minn.: Capstone Press, 2008.

Internet Sites

FactHound offers a safe, fun way to find Internet sites related to this book. All of the sites on FactHound have been researched by our staff.

Here's all you do:

Visit *www.facthound.com*

Type in this code: 9781429675833

Super-cool stuff!

Check out projects, games and lots more at
www.capstonekids.com

23

Index

Word Count: 217

Grade: 1

Early-Intervention Level: 22